Tell The World

Understanding Oneself

Stephen Jahseed Lark

Use Your QR App
To Learn More Today

Table of Contents

I'm not writing this book to make money as money has failed to make me happy during this lifetime.

For right now, at least on this day of April 8th, 2009, I do not have a job because I quit mine years ago when I was making about $30,000 a year.

Now, you might be thinking to yourself, "How sad..."

Or, depending on your level of consciousness, you might be thinking, "How freeing..."

But really, I am extremely grateful and happy to not be working—or, should I say, not having to stress over the problems that come with working today.

I did these things because I didn't want to lose myself in this world. I did not want to create a false persona and be in so deep that I couldn't get myself back to who I needed to be, which is pure consciousness...

I did this for myself, so I can create a family that's not taught hand-me-down beliefs from past generations. I did this, so I can raise my children in a world of pure, unconditional love and consciousness. I will write more conscious books and maybe films someday...

This is what I see for myself and family, and others as well. But it all starts with me. This is my destiny. I must tell the world...

Being my first book, and I'm taking a leap to do this. I don't know how far this will get me, but there're too many people who said, "You can't do it, and you'll never make it as a young author or writer." This is my dream, my reality, and I'll follow my heart. So now I'm doing it. I really hope that this nation will be quicker to listen to the true nature of love than to judge...

I love to write and would love to travel all over the world someday. But even with all this freedom, there's still something missing....

What is that?

Well, I'll tell you...

A series of books that I call...

"Tell the world!"

Let me just briefly explain how I got to this point: It all started when I was first introduced to this movie called "The Secret" in 2007...

It was kind of funny how I stumbled across this movie. I worked at Hollywood Video as a store director, and one day I was closing the store. My hands were like a magnet when I got close to the movie.

After I took the video home and watched it, I was astonished at how every thought of mine fit into place as this movie projected. It was like a piece of a puzzle that I had been looking for all my life I had just found…

I quickly started manifesting things in my life, such as a better job, a new car, and my own apartment. All this happened within a one year, but as soon as I obtained those things, I became unhappy…

It seemed like I was not happy with myself. I was still building up a false persona. I was drowning myself with guilt, with bogus money. The economy was getting bad and the nation was heading into a recession, but I was not even feeling it. Now I know what you are thinking: "You are making money, and you're not happy? How crazy!"

You're right. It was not affecting me at all. Yet some part of me was affected and that was my soul. My soul wasn't happy, and I knew this. So I quit my job and wanted to do something better with myself.

In the year of 2009, I decided to write my first book, *Tell the World*, and in due time, I would love to write many new books and movies about consciousness.…

I've been meditating on this and, I know that the God that lives in me and in all of us—and also this entire universe—wants me to do this. I have no choice. My life is dedicated to this. I must… *Tell the World*!

This society is going in a very peculiar way. I know that this book will not only help you live your dream, but also explain why the nation is going in the direction it is, and how every human being needs to empower themselves everyday through meditation. Stop letting the judgments of the human mind get the best of you…

Before I begin, let me first say that I know in my heart that many people will accuse me of blasphemy. They'll even curse me. Many people will not like me after everything is said and done, but I am still excited. That is just the way the world works—for now, at least.

But the way I look at it, people have been doing that all my life, including my own family.

So, it is really nothing new to me.

I have been different all my life. I look at myself as the black sheep of the family.

I used to take abuse from every angle and aspect from unconscious human beings.

So, coming out with this book has not only inspired me to enhance my ability to become more of who I am but also this process has shown me who has my back and who doesn't.

A lot of what I'm releasing will make people uncomfortable. But let's face it: Many parts of the world are uncomfortable, so this should be interesting reading for many of us.

I feel like the world needs to know this truth: We are God experiencing life on a physical plane. The world can be a better place to live. I really believe that this is Heaven on Earth, but I also believe that it's probably too late for a lot of changes because God's will is at hand.

A change is coming to the world, and we are seeing it happen. Seems like with just a blink of an eye, so much is evolving: same sex marriage, tsunamis, crooked government power, economic slavery, children getting slaughtered and used in sex acts, animals getting slaughtered and used in sex acts, famine, plagues, wildfires, storms, earthquakes, volcanic eruptions, mind control, and the evolution of consciousness, etc.....

This is only the beginning of what's to come. It sounds scary, but it is not. This is a change that affects every last one of us. We all have to get closer to our supreme self—which is living inside each and every last one of us—to understand this cosmic change. We can't let the outside world manipulate our minds. That leads to a quicker death.

I know that in the beginning of this book I said that my spirit was affected. What I really meant is my soul would not allow me to stay asleep, to continue contributing to unconscious thinking and ways. I say this because when you get to a place of stillness within the mind and body, it's impossible to continue with habits of unawareness. They cease to exist.

"Know thyself" or understanding who you are can be challenging for many believe me it was for me. That is what this first book is about, along with other things. And it's going to be fun writing this book because I know that there aren't that many books out there that talk about the things that aren't taught, lectured, or preached. That's what excites me. I know, within my heart, that there're many light entities out there on this earth that feel the exact same way that I do about this world. We're a mirror to each and every last one of us. We're all one. And last, but not least, the universe is expanding, and the light species that we are is rising fast....

Now before I move forward, let me tell you that what I am about to release to you is not from Stephen Lark. Yes, I'm writing this, but the human body is numbed while writing this book. These aren't thoughts arising in my brain. I'm completely one. "God or (Jahseed) has taken complete control," for I am Jahseed...

Stephen Lark is a human being. The name was given to me by man. I had no choice in the matter. In fact, no one came to me and said, "What would you like your name to be?"

My name is Jahseed Astronomous, which is my choice of God. Many people may not agree with who I choose to be into his life but I can't run from the fact that I am aware.

This is the grandest way to live. If it does not start with one person, it will not be so. It'll only be a thought, and now is the time for this thought to be a reality. For what I perceive through my mind is what I perceive through my eyes and what I perceive through my eyes is what I perceive through my mind.

Understanding one's self should always be in effect at all times and should stay in effect for all our lifetimes, so we may arise as a species of light beings.

There're many of us out there. Now is the time for everyone to stop ignoring the fact that it is inevitable.

This is the true nature of the man and woman (god/goddess).

Many people do not see themselves as a god/goddess. But, by the time you are done with this book, I know you'll have the understanding that you're something more than just an ordinary human being.

Ok, now that we have that out of the way, let us finish:

There're many things that I want to talk about in this first book, so people can understand where this world can go if we continue living without understanding why we're here.

Nobody will know what direction this world is going until we, as a whole, realize that we've been taught the wrong lesson about ourselves as a human species. We must recognize the true essence of who we are, and that is the supreme self. We ought to understand there's a great deal of stillness that needs to be in place in one's heart, mind, and body. We will lose more precious souls if we do not work on this.

Some unfortunate souls aren't lost in the presence of being present. They're lost within their mind—attached to thoughts and emotions.

I've found out who I am. I'm very thankful for the other gods/goddesses who have brought me to this reality of being, such as Michael Beckwith, Lisa Nichols, Alan Watts, Neal Donald Walsh, Ronna Herman, Joel Goldsmith, Mary and Ester Hicks, Rajinder Singh, Eckhart Tolle, Deepak Chopra, Don Miguel Ruiz, Jiddu Krishnamurti plus many more. The books that I've been reading by these remarkable authors are so exciting and freeing. I have not met these remarkable beings in person, but someday, maybe I will…

That's what leads me to write, and also to be free to enjoy my life. Everybody should be free and full of joy, love, and peace of mind. We've a chance to create our own kingdom of happiness. That's the right we all have as a light species.

I believe that for all of humanity, life is meant to be happy. If you do not believe that, then keep reading on. Hopefully you will see after reading the next couple of pages…

If you're on the level of not wanting to step out of the box or not wanting to fall into the rabbit hole or of wanting to stay asleep, then you probably won't be able to comprehend what I'm saying. In other words, the mind must be still and vibrate at the same level in which these words are emerging. Some paragraphs may be too deep to handle. But I guarantee, by the time you finish this book, some part (or parts) of you will not be the same.

This book is not intended to change anyone's views about themselves or get anyone to reshape their reality. This book is from the heart of the world and the entire universe...

Change is not for everybody all the time. You must mature, to be open to change. If you want eternal life, good food for the mind, good health, a beautiful relationship, maybe a better job, or even just to laugh and prosper, keeping reading this book. You'll be transformed not because you are forced, but because you are the supreme self.

I will make it plain and simple so that even a child can understand. This book is very simple, because not everybody likes to read, and, also, life is just that simple....

Okay. Here we go:

You are the most conscious as a child....

Now as you pay attention to your surroundings, you become more and more aware of human behavior...

Why is that?

We've all been taught these false and negative feelings of life, such as anger, fear, terrorism, jealousy, envy, pride, worries, condemnation, hate, etc.

We pick these feelings up by judging every situation and by holding every situation captive in our memory.

So, the next time a situation appears in your presence, you judge the present moment situation as you did before—whatever the situation may be.

These feelings don't exist in a world of pure consciousness. They only exist in a world of hate, violence, wars, condemnation, judgments, and punishments. Some people may call this total suffering and reactionary consciousness Hell.

Our minds hold onto every event we look at as "normal life situations," but truly they are opportunities for learning who we truly are. These events start with:

Your "thinking."

Oh, it gets better…

We remember these events. When they pop up again in different form but the same event, you react by memory and judgments from the last time the event arose.

You judge the same event and act out and react out again and again and again until you become conscious and aware of that event and start to look at it from a conscious—or should I say oneness? —point of view. And then you get it, but by that time you may be 75 or 60 or 88 or 92 or even 23 or 28 or 19 or 15. The age does not really matter. What does matter is your level of consciousness.

The situation does not affect you anymore, because you know who you are: You're the situation itself.

Let me add that by being parents and going to many, many institutions—in dealing with today's society—that some of us don't have a choice, but we all learn how to behave.

We all play a part in these acts, whether we know it or not, by doing what I call the "norm" or living day-by-day. This is how we pick up human behavior…

Unconsciousness is all in the mind. We can wake up.…

But before I get into how this can happen, let me just tell the world about…

1

Distractions

What has become a distraction for you?

In order to become more aware of the god that you are right now, you have to know what is in the forefront of your reality. What comes first in your dreams?

You're reading this book right now, so that tells you that your self is primary for you and that's the first step in knowing that you're God. You always have to take care of home first. Home is where the heart is. Always remember that.

If you have that in heart, you will never fail.

Always take care of yourself first, because you can't help anyone else unless you help yourself first. You're the first step in following your destiny—not your mom, not your dad, not your children, not anyone. Nobody can help you figure you out but you.

We all know what distraction means: anything that takes away from you focusing on yourself or reaching your true nature. It can be a person, place, or thing.

So, again: What has become a distraction for you?

Let us do something for a quick minute...

Close your eyes and try to shut down all thoughts. Now, just think about what has become a distraction for you. The distraction for you... is...

What is blocking you from reaching your true God self.

You see that you've a lot of distractions in your world. What are you going to do next?

Let me help you out.

Nothing!

You cannot make the decision out of flesh; the decision must come from the unknown. Otherwise, you'll always fall back into the hands of your own misery...

Look at it this way: the minute you rush out and try to commit to anything out of unconsciousness, you're not in control. You may think you are, but you're not. The false you—ego—is doing all the work.

Yes, the ego!

You know what I am talking about: the person that you think you are, the mind that you listen to day after day after day, the mind that you mistake for...well, for yourself...

I mean your false sense of self or being that you've built up, because you do not know who you are. You have replaced thoughts and memory to fill that hole.

You mistake memories and thoughts as the entity that you are. You fool yourself.

Many, many, many gods/goddesses have talked about this total consciousness. If you don't look at the next person as yourself, you're living backward because you separate yourself from the life you are.

You really do not know who you are... or maybe you do!

You just choose not to listen.

Listen to who or what?

Listening to your real self. Some people may call that "super conscious," but I call it the God self.

This voice is the same voice that's releasing these words on this page right now. It's the voice that speaks to you all the time, but you have to shut down all the other noise in your head first in order to get to the real voice (the voice from the unknown or divine source).

The unknown?

The unknown is a mystical place from which everything is known such as real knowledge, truth, ecstasy, love, and wisdom—this is the place from which all those attributes are born...

Can we get to this place?

The answer is yes and that's through meditation, which will lead to stilling the body and mind...

Now the voice, on the other hand, is your own voice. But you don't listen to this voice only, since you have other voices in your head that you've built up from past lifetimes and also through the present lifetime as well.

You must clear these voices out because, if you don't, you'll wander here—not in beauty—but in your world of Hell forever.

You'll never experience the real beauty of yourself, nor anyone around you, until you look at the other people with the perception that you're looking at yourself. Or let me put it this way: You make it harder for the beauty of Earth to be marveled at by humans because you're un-aware. Not realizing who or what you are holds you and everybody else back. You continue to spread this disease among others. Lack of awareness is a poison to you and to the people around you.

The unknown, however—well, let's put it this way: When you medi-tate, not only do you have to slow the thoughts of the mind down, but you actually have to stop thinking. Thinking equals movement. In or-der for the mind to live, it must live on thoughts. It's how we operate.

You must stop thinking, so you can allow the unknown to step in. You have to slow down your breathing as well. As you breathe slower, you will require less oxygen.

This is an art. Don't get me wrong. It might sound kind of stupid, but it brings you to a place that you'll always look forward to going to. You will not need drugs or acceptance from other people. That's how good meditation is for the human species.

If you ask me, for many people, the number one distraction is the mind!

Look at it this way: You have at least 60,000 thoughts a day. And when you are not aware of it, it is impossible to slow the mind down because you're interacting with society, and you have to keep moving in order to be normal. That is how you are programed.

You have to think about this and think about that. You're always on the move, never having the time to rest, intentionally breathe, or even focus on one thing at a time. That's how life can be a program. Maybe this is your life...

But if you do not break away from it, you'll never understand who or what you are...

All your actions are committed under in unawareness. It may seem like, at this very minute, that it is working. It looks good, but with the blink of an eye, your world is turned upside down. You did not see it coming. You were blind and not aware of your surroundings. So now you are back to step one, depending on your level of consciousness. You get to blame everything on everybody...

Stop pointing the finger. Anytime you see anything in anybody else, it is what you see in yourself. You are "the man in the mirror." I call it the mirror effect, which is another reason you're not supposed to judge anyone, anything, or anybody. You will only find out later that you are judging yourself.

Try to understand this: You're reading this book because you're energy made into flesh—human form—and you've attracted everything into your life because you're like a magnet.

Energy attracts energy; negative attracts negative; and positive attracts positive!

Whenever you get this down in the root of your living, you'll break away from everything you were taught. You will find out that everything is a lie, including what you are wearing right now.

Understand that you're living in a dream. You can do any and everything you always wanted to do. Snap out of this dream of not knowing what's going on. You are life.

Yes. You're life. You create life in anything and everything you do by your thoughts, feelings, and actions. Merging all three together brings forth your reality, good or bad.

Do you get it now?

You must understand this if you want to change your dream.

I say this. (Stop resisting!)

That's what you're doing right now: resisting. If you keep resisting, you'll never move on to the next level. Open up your mind and let go. When you resist the present moment, you cut yourself off from what's truly going on. You look at everything as an obstacle, not realizing that things happen because they do. There's nothing too serious!

Ever!

Not once has anything been too serious for this truth. And that's what resisting does—it blinds you from the truth. So again, I say, "Let go."

Know the distraction. Fix the distraction, not by force but by you…

Replace yourself with knowledge of knowing yourself…

This is why, when your level of consciousness starts to emerge, you begin to lose friends. Not everybody will immediately think like you, act like you, or even compare to your knowledge. They'll all turn their heads and say bogus things about you. They'll mock you and tell lies, all because you've changed. In fact, you are not behaving yourself anymore. You're acting out nature: being nature...

You can't fail at the life you are. It's impossible to fail. The only reason you fail—or you feel like you fail—is because, given your state of mind, you see it that way. Your world will begin to crumble because you're creating failure through your thoughts, feelings, and actions...

You've the thought of failure and the feeling of failure. What is next? It leads to producing failure and your reality becoming your Hell...

Everything you do will be negative because you're the one who produced it—not anybody else, whatever the situation may look like.

Remember this, "Nothing matters but the state you're in. You're evolving constantly, day by day, and all you have is your feeling. Your feeling will take you wherever you desire to go, so know thyself"...

Never ever forget that, if you desire to learn anything about the life you are, just remember that. Then you'll live a long and prosperous existence.

Always stay positive, so when events happen that try to break you down, you are already in the positive state.

Any "supposedly negative" event should be looked at positively.

If you treat a situation with a negative action, it'll produce negative results. Positive actions will produce positive results.

Whatever you put out comes right back to you because we're energy, and energy sends out energy and then receives energy. If you're emitting negative energy, you'll receive negative events. Likewise, if you're emitting positive energy, you'll receive positive events.

Events are speeded up by your vibrations. Vibrations are pockets of energy that create energy. So if you're energy, which makes up energy, with pockets of vibration, just one little idea of success will bring you your world of success. It only takes one minute of focus—on the idea of whatever you see yourself accomplishing—to bring forth new ideas that create your world.

Everything that I am saying is the "universal law." They don't even teach this in schools, churches, seminars, etc. If you put this law to the test, I can guarantee that you'll be transformed.

You can determine who you really are by not judging any situation, not recognizing anything as good or bad; just see it as it is...

"The is-ness of life, the yin-yang effect, that's plain black and white for you..."

Know who you are. The quicker you get this, the quicker you'll be free from anxiety, sickness, mixed emotions, judgment, and the chaos of the mind. Decide quickly. The evolution of consciousness is emerging faster than you think. You do not want to be left out in the cold or should I say the old world.

President Barack Obama said that a change is coming. He's right. A change is coming. I am not sure Obama meant the change I've in mind, however. The change I'm talking about is a change of the mind—like doing something different, thinking outside of the box, not doing what you see everybody else doing, not being attached to desire or protection:

A change of consciousness!

You must escape the flock of sheep. Realize, "Hey. I don't have to do what he or she is doing. I'm going to do my own thing." If you do that, then you'll be reroute to self-discovery, exploring your true essence. Believe it or not, you're in this by yourself.

The reason that there're more people on the same journey is because of the expansion of the universe.

Be different. Be very different. Do not imitate the people you see on the television. You should not desire to be like any person out in the world but yourself...

Many mystics have pointed out that we're here in the world, but guard against being of the world unconsciously. What you perceive through your eyes is nothing but an illusion.

You're in control of your own destiny. There're many distractions out there to destroy you—to stop you in your very path—but "who you are" is the key to "knowing the distraction." With that knowledge, prosperity comes in every form possible.

2

Human Beings

Have you ever been employed, and you said to yourself? "

I wish I could find another job," or thought, "

They don't pay me enough for what I do," or wished for a vacation?

I did on January 1st, 2009. Let me briefly explain:

I was working at Chase credit card service, making about $25,000 a year (not much).

At the time, all I had was me, my son, and my pregnant girlfriend.

I gave up a one bedroom apartment to move in with my girlfriend and son. I eventually got evicted because I lacked a job.

Was I happy with what I was doing?

I had to ask myself that question and the answer was, "No."

I was making the money, but I wasn't happy. It was like dying.

I was doing the right thing for my family, but it was killing me. I wanted to be happy for both me and my family—not just my family. If one part of a relationship is off, then the whole relationship is off.

I was happy, but happiness was not in the life that I am...

I'd finally made it to a point where I could meditate for hours and relax and enjoy this reality. All I wanted to do was read, read, read, and study about living in the now.

I wanted to travel and speak to everyone who knew about happiness and being present in the now. At this time of my life, I can full say I have achieved happiness and Freedom.

Total freedom.

That is what I came up with, which leads me to question:

What is total freedom?

To me, total freedom arises from not having to stress and run around like a chicken with your head cut off, trying to make ends meet. Total freedom is "living your destiny."

Everybody can sit back and think about living their true dream and following their destiny.

Whatever situation you are in, always follow your heart. Follow your destiny, whatever it is. Once you start to follow your destiny, then all unconscious events will immediately dissipate. I guarantee you this.

"Follow your heart and stay focused on your primary objective ..."

Human beings worry about bills. They stress about how their kids are going to get a college education. They stress when they don't have food in the house, and so on.

We all must be who we are in every way possible. We cannot let ego dwell in others' judgments.

So, I finally asked myself,

"Why's it like that?"

Why do so many humans stress, stress, stress and live as if they have no destiny?

The answer is this:

They're only human beings!

First off, I want to define human being:

A human being is a lost spirit who's been physically born from a woman. It loses its spiritual consciousness as it matures from a child to an adult.

In other words, as a child you're one of the most conscious beings there are, some more than others. A child is a recent incarnation of a god or goddess.

Children seek love and are unafraid of life. It's as you become more and more aware of "the dangers of life" that you lose touch with being...

Parenting can be one of the most dangerous roles to play if you still operate in human being unconsciousness.

Why? You expect everything to be right. You lose the understanding that chaos will always be around, no matter what. These acts of turmoil are caused only from the negative energetic forces that the unconscious mind produces.

We have to give ourselves the title of parent to act out the role. We assume the function of a parent should be over-protective and controlling, but we've all failed to realize that our kids are not really our kids.

Do not take anything too seriously, not even your own life.

Anyone can see that when you take this life too seriously, it'll let you down. Everything is based on the monetary system. With that in place, there's division between humans. The monetary system has no room for self-development. It is always going to be about the money.

We're created upon feeling and love. There's no doubt about that. Every event that happens to us creates either a negative or positive feeling. Money, on the other hand, creates short-term happiness. Money isn't an infinite resource. It comes and goes. If you live for the value of money, then you'll never find happiness. It is that simple.

Many people are lost, in one way or another. Their thoughts are lost. They don't know who they truly are.

That is not to say that you do not know who you are, but you define yourself as a human being and that is one way we all lose ourselves.

The materialist thought of, "I'm my body," needs to be broken for the safety of humanity and to bring forth new levels of consciousness.

A new level of consciousness needs to evolve that will further the lifespan of humanity. The way society is going now, we're killing ourselves. We lack self-exploration and meditation. We partake in unconscious institutions. We work at stressful jobs, only to pay off loans, bills, houses, and cars. To sum it all up, you build up assets to conform to society's lifestyle.

If you died right now, all the things you had would not matter. Why would it matter? The body that was present is no longer alive. Consciousness has basically left the building…

I do not reject that we are human. I'm trying to say we need to lose the title of human being. We're in a body made of matter, but that's not it. We're still gods/goddesses in the inside and out. We're pure gold manifested into human form. We're the universe. We were created for the expansion of the universe.

This is what should be the primary concern of all human beings. But it is not. Tell me: Why is that?

Are you living in a highly structured society? Do you feel like you cannot get out of this box?

Let us talk about that box:

Your thinking causes chaos. There's a way out of this turmoil, however, and it all starts with the stillness of the mind. Without stillness—with only constant, hectic change to guide your mind—you'll perceive life as Hell.

When you define yourself as a human being, you lose touch with spirit. You lose touch with the diamond awaiting inside of you—the diamond waiting to be manifested into the light of pure consciousness. Love will be the end of all corruption.

It is okay. Believe me. I'm not saying our teaching of humanity is wrong wholesale, but I'm attempting to point out that there's a drastically negative aspect to it: You pick up qualities of the human behavior instead of your inner God-nature.

Human behavior—or unconsciousness—causes anger, judgment, greed, lying, fear, anxiety, scams, corruption of the mind, the need to control, mocking, pride, killing, and the list of ills goes on and on and on…

Human nature, or consciousness, conversely, equates to oneness with all: love, truth, honesty, kindness, longevity, energy, bliss, pure knowledge born of ecstasy, and so on…

Anybody should be able to understand this, but not everybody does because we do not take the time out of our busy days to study who we truly are or even to meditate. All we do as humans is judge. We watch television so our minds can continue to get fed garbage. We work to pay off assets. And we get angry when things do not go our way. We unconsciously kill ourselves due to our ignorance regarding the self.

Get back to your true essence. Get back to consciousness. Follow your heart. Stop doubting yourself. If you hear a voice in your head encouraging you to move forward, then stop procrastinating and get the job done. Listening to the wrong voice will result in a Hell on Earth, rather than the accessible Heaven.

"Knowing who you are on the inside equals extra knowledge for the outside…"

"The soul needs to be fed if you want to get ahead."

If you always keep that knowledge in thought, then I guarantee, by the end of your lifetime, you'll experience true unconditional love—not from another person, but true unconditional love from God, the Supreme Self.

Many people meditate. It's one of the first signs of discovering who you are. Sadly, to this day, many people can't control their minds or even slow down enough to meditate for one minute.

Why is that so?

We are worried about what is going to happen next. We worry about what is the next move. We almost play chess in our heads. We live life thought after thought after thought after thought...

You know what I am talking about. "What's the weather going to be like tomorrow? Am I dressed for the occasion? The kids have to go to bed. The wife or husband is almost home. I ought to run the bathwater. Do I have clean socks? I should exercise to please my spouse. Man, I would like to watch television. I got to do this and that. Which holiday is coming up next?" It seems like there's always another thought about to appear!

Desire and attachment is always needing to cling to something. I know it can be hard to internalize what I'm relating as wisdom for your life. Language is not the best conveyer of these truths; life is. But I know I can help you see.

We all go back and forth with renouncing the past and the future. Believe me: We all do this, whether we know it or not. That is the conditioning of the mind at work... not a mind of your own.

This is happening only because you're allowing it to happen. You know that this's correct, otherwise you would not be reading this book. There should be very deep vibrations emanating from you as you read this book. That is the feeling you should live for always.

The human mind is a working muscle that's always differentiating between "reality and false reality," "real or not real," "the truth and the lie." This is what the mind does always. What are you doing to control your mind? Do not resist the present moment.

Give yourself a minute to contemplate this.

Regain who you are—no matter what. It is imperative that you do this. You are a god manifested in a human, energetic form. Please do not resist this truth.

Allow yourself to be submerged into truth; allow yourself to be present in the moment; allow yourself to hear, without labeling what you hear. Allow yourself to heal, with the knowledge of understanding. Feel the energy that you possess as you emerge into oneness with the mind and body. Breathe, allowing everything that you think of "to be as is," with no emotional attachment and no main focus of attention. Allow each thought to be pure on its own. Allow the feeling to be born from within you, so that you know everything is born from thought. You're the decider of its right destiny.

God is everyone, everybody and everything.

The mind can't handle what it can't experience as total reality. The mind judges reality by the senses. O ahead and Watch the (tell-your-vision) and judge what you see. It will not hurt you. "Feed me; feed me," that is what the unconscious mind is saying always.

So now you are lost—not because you want to be—but because you unconsciously chose to be lost...

Let me put it this way: You're a zombie! You are the walking dead. Imagine that! TV *is* good for something.

Learn to laugh. I am trying to wake you up here.

You do not take the time out of your day to get to know who you are on the inside. To me, that's equivalent to saying you're not worthy to live.

I don't mean to be rude, but it's the truth.

You must take time each and every day to study your inner self, to train the mind to be still. This isn't an overnight process. This is a second nature process... and that is how it will feel. The sooner that you see it, the sooner you will be free.

You must meditate to get to know your inner self. If you seek on the outside for self, you will only get outside results that are due to fail.

The outside—or should I say the world—is an illusion of what's going on in your mind. If you have chaos in the mind, you'll definitely produce chaos through your eyes. What you see is what you get. Constantly having stillness within the mind and body will lift you to a level of purity. And the world you perceive within that stillness has already proven to be a paradise in your presence.

You choose to go to work for over 40 hours a week.

You choose to go to church, temple or mosque and listen to what the so-called "authorities" tell you: your priest, reverend, minister, rabbi, imam, pastor, or pope...

Why do you do these things? Do you really believe they have the answer?

If you have been seeking for longer than your age, then it is time for a change. You see, enlightenment is not something that has been hidden. It's been there all along. We just chose not to listen...

You've assigned a parental role to yourself and others.

You've forced yourself to believe that life is about going to school, finishing college, paying bills, paying taxes, going to church, finding a job, etc....

Many, many, many people are so lost due to the lack of meditation, but now—and right now! —is the time for this society and this nation to wake up and see themselves as the Supreme Self.

The knowledge of this is so simple to grasp. Can we really afford to embark on another decade full of lost, imperial minds?

The human species won't survive without the realization of self, without the knowledge that we're the Supreme Self of this universe, without the stillness of the mind, without the evolution of thought, without the love of our being, without the knowledge that with every breath we breathe, we breathe abundance to our essence of being. We're all...

What does that tell you?

The fact that you're here on this Earth as a human isn't some mistake...

It is simply miraculous, whether you know it or not...

Everything is in a rush to become a human being because of the many miraculous qualities we have. Being unaware, you are oblivious to all the knowledge present here. You cannot even grasp the full potential of human nature, because this is what you want. You are asking to be small until you separate yourself from all the world's delusions. Do not separate yourself from others.

We can imagine a society free of pain, suffering, sorrow, enslavement, and governmental power. It's agreed upon that we've all the resources to take care of each and every person on Earth. Peace can be attained. Unity is at hand. Everything is simply just a footstep away. What's the problem?

People, wake up! You can hear, touch, taste, smell, see, and even experience sexual feelings among other gods and goddesses.

That is the blessing that has been created by being here in a body made of matter. We all need to acknowledge that the human being experience is real as far as its qualities are in fact experienced. But do not lose focus on your primary nature, which is pure, unconditional, God love.

I say this because you've the ability to experience whoever you want to become…

"Live the life you are for you and no one else but you."

When you live for somebody else, you simply die. It is like committing suicide, because you are not you…

You are not authentic…

You're just simply creating a clone of the other person—or capturing a clone of universal thoughts unconsciously. You must build a sense of me. "This is who I am through the mind of past and future." You never seem to grasp that past and future is now. You live as if you're here to get old and die. That isn't a good way to live. We're all eternal. Death is only a means to a return…

And never forget that.

That is why so many people act out of unconscious human behavior instead out of conscious human nature.

Remember that you're creating who you are every second, minute, and hour of your life. You're creating your world through your thoughts, feelings, and actions (through your mind, soul, and body).

Know who you are. If you do not yet, then that is okay. Your time is coming quicker than you think. Life comes and goes, but the soul is eternal and will always find its way towards nirvana.

We all should focus on our inner selves. We need to empower the soul, no matter what. Show true, unconditional love by helping others to see the proper way to live. That is what we are here for. Not to just live and worry about ourselves, but to pull each other up as well…

Humans is only how we have defined ourselves. However, the soul or spirit is the true nature of the human species.

Let us act out our nature, because negative human behavior is what is giving the human race its bad name. Plenty of times on this planet, humans even fail to recognize itself. That is where any type of thought, feeling, or action lacks the basis of what should be our existence: Love.

3

Religion...

It makes me laugh so hard that you can say that you're so many separate entities...

In other words, how can you say you're Baptist, Pentecostal, Muslim, Catholic, or even Buddhist—just to name a few?

They all say the same thing, teach the same lessons, and pray to the same God....

Don't you know that when you label yourself, you're dividing yourself? Why divide up your race? In so doing, you will take away a piece of who you are.

You don't even seek the other religions. Instead, you mock the other religions and curse your neighbor because of their different beliefs. "You're a little gang."

Religion is a business and a hoax. It's not useful, only selfishness, greed, wanting of material assets, stubbornness, hate for other souls, war, politics, killings, judging and so on and so forth...

The church is supposed to represent the body of all. People go around with a church consciousness, spreading it. Everybody has an opinion, but what really matters is who has their own thoughts.

That's why there's so much chaos in the world. There's too much chaos in our minds. Whose voice do you hear in your head when you do things? "You do things because you do things." You are trying to learn who you are. You are trying to determine if there's anything wrong with this. "Do I have free will?" When you're exploring yourself, anything and everything you do is right, yet you also must experience what's called wrong—negative, the bad side, evil, whatever label you'd prefer—you have to go through these events in order to experience life. Everything we see are possibilities. Consciousness chooses between these possibilities. That's creation for you.

Let us get back to who we really are: God/goddess consciousness.

When you establish yourself as religious, then you're truly saying that you're two separate entities.

You're two people battling about who you really are.

What we do not know is that we all do this battling in one way or another.

You try to identify yourself as so many identities instead of the one identity which is Consciousness.

Yes. I said it. And I know some of you can't grasp that. I told you that this book would be good. You're the very creator of the life you are. You're that big bang of love.

Put the human body under a microscope, look down to the minutest speck, and what do you see? Energy, which equals light...

You've emerged out of the darkness and into the light. The god/goddess is made from energy—or should I say light?—so there you have it! You're the Supreme Self. This is the great secret that nobody wants to say, but now is the time for all of humanity to hear the voice of truth. Let the ones who have ears, hear. Let any being that has a mind use it for the greatest good for humanity.

The truth is in you all!

We identify ourselves as teacher, parent, mother, father, pastor, counselor, doctor, dentist, lawyer, policemen, women, or even the president of a country. All of these definitions are illusions of the mind you inhabit. We need to see past these illusions, because we can get stuck. It is easy to get caught in the tentacles of this dream. They are just passing thoughts from the universal mind—fun illusions of what the mind can imagine. But it is paramount that we do not forget how to return to the Supreme Self...

Have fun with your life. Do not take it too seriously.

Sometimes a thought will motivate you to experience something unconsciously. Sometimes, conscious thoughts will motivate you to an action too, depending on your level of consciousness.

For example, you might be very sexual, having prevalent thoughts of being with tons of women or men. Then you may inhabit the ego of a porn artist, pimp, or player unconsciously.

Unconscious thoughts can get you into a heap of trouble, if you do not know who you are.

Unconscious thoughts can be hazardous to your health, an endangerment to your life as a god/goddess.

With these thoughts held in your mind, you will be led to wealth, tons of women or men, diseases, or maybe even a quicker death.

You've simply lost connection with who you really are, which is a god/goddess.

You can have goals and ambitions. There is nothing wrong with that. In fact, there is so much right with that—as long as you remember who you really are.

When you obtain these worldly images of what seems to be materially prosperous, you will only get results of what these chaotic unconscious thoughts bring forth, which is a quicker death...

Whether you like it or not!

Now let us address religion in more depth. When you embrace any religion, you are confusing yourself for something smaller than you are.

Religion equals uncertainty.

I laugh at the thought of being separate from anybody. You should too! I am everybody and everything. So are you. Nice to meet you.

From the plant growing in the ground to the clouds in the air, we are all.

"I am all..."

Religion has nothing to do with who you are.

Religion is only a signpost of who is and what is on a never-ending, but complete, road.

That's why human beings constantly battle against one religion or another any given day. There are so many emotions and thoughts of the past that make-up religion. You subsume that history, acting as if these thoughts are your personality (but it's only a fraction of you).

Hold onto the idea that you're not your body and see what comes about. I dare you.

There're so many faces of religion, but only one true aspect of it exists today.

It's always been around, but human beings still reject it:

Energy is all there is.

Jesus knew this, but humans rejected him.

We do not want to believe this truth, but it is all there is.

We want to believe in all the other faces of religion, but not the truth.

We want to believe what every priest, pope, preacher, minister, deacon, sister, brother, mother, son, daughter—whoever you may listen to—says about religion, but not hear what the truth is. Energy is all there is. Know this and you will be free...

I found out the truth, and I was instantly free in just the blink of an eye... Oh, yes, I became free from the ego, that false sense of self— finally free from the unconscious mind running my life, free from being religious, free from blindly accepting the opinions of religious people, free from the illusion of time. I became free from the mind.

I did not have to feel low in life because I didn't go to college or continue to work at unconscious institutions. I felt higher and lighter as soon as I dropped the expectations.

I'm not saying that I'm perfect. But I'm certainly saying that we're all perfect in every way possible. It may not seem that way, but that's the truth. God is me; god is you; and god is all. Knowing this is truth and freedom...

The truth will always set you free...

You're the truth.

Only your soul—or your inner energy-light being—can understand this knowledge, but every being on the face of this planet has a soul. It is not hard to recognize this truth, since it lives within the roots of life.

Just meditate for just a couple of minutes with your eyes closed. Shut down every thought that appears to come in your head. Don't think about anything, swallow, twitch, move, answer the phone, or do anything for just three minutes. Use an alarm clock if you need to. Then say to yourself before the three minutes start, "Am I happy with the job I've got and the friends that I've made. Who am I without anything?"

Are you done? If so, then great. If not, stop reading for three minutes and return. I will always be waiting here.

Let go of all worldly possessions and reveal the truth.

Will you survive with only yourself?

Why is it that you've nothing to do, but to identify yourself as a separate individual?

TELL THE WORLD

Are you satisfied with the results you're getting?

If not, then change it!

Start to identify yourself as god/goddess and see the results you get...

I dare you.

What else do you have to lose at this point?

Everything else has proven to fail.

It seems like you're afraid of what might become of you, which is nothing.

Lose the very aspect of who you think you are and what do you have?

You've nothing!

You may lose all of your friends, but that means they weren't your friends in the first place. They were "ego attachers," as I call them. As long as you were acting out of unconsciousness, they were around. But that is okay, because you'll gain new friends. You will find friends of the new thought, friends that'll care for you, friends that will help you out no matter what. Why? Because you are your friends and your friends are you.

"You create your reality only because you are reality. So the reality of your mind tells your story..."

You also gain something else: meditation. This is very important. Without it, we cannot understand our true energy-filled selves. I cannot stress this enough. But I realize one lives their own life with their own beliefs...

Stillness is the first language of the god/goddess.

You also gain true knowledge from ecstasy and true wisdom born from formless thought.

Love is the key to every known being on Earth.

Love will carry you to the depths of the sea.

Love will take you to every direction of the universe: north, south, east and west.

Love is all there is—love among the gods and goddesses—if you want to sum it together.

Love feels like the presence of death, which is such a beautiful state to experience.

But I do not want to get off track. That is a whole new book to come...

Do not get caught up in being religious or being in a certain religion.

All religions have proven to be a truth and a lie...

Some know the truth and some do not, but the lie is that the truth is not all said to be true.

So, with all, then what else is there?

Feeling, "for feeling is the nature of the soul" ... (Neal Donald Walsh)

Just know that the soul's nature is your true nature. You're the soul, not the body. The body dies; the soul doesn't. Can you sense that there's truth within what you're reading?

Feeling is the key to truth...

Feeling is the nature of the soul...

Feeling has always been the nature of the soul and the nature of our hearts. Feeling is one of the processes by which we got here.

You are your soul or spirit or god. It's all the same.

You do not have to go to a church to relieve your poverty.

You can feel wealthy on the inside. You can get yourself out of poverty because it is a state of mind. There's no such thing as poverty. The instant you realize wealth isn't material, you activate that crystalline light in which all must obey your command.

You can pray and tithe and give all your money to the churches yet still find yourself incomplete. Go to the inside of self and find that spark of light, that spark of love, bliss, and ecstasy. You will then begin to emerge from the state of sleeplessness...

You must feel who you are. You cannot find who you are in a preacher, pastor, reverend, or pope. You find out who you are by yourself and by people in general (not titles).

Do not worship any other man for your well-being. God has given each of us what we need. Of course this is true, but when you falsely acknowledge a man you give him a sense of false importance about himself. Follow your heart. Don't follow any other man but yourself, because that's where god/goddess lives: in you.

Religion is a political fact. That is why many of the sons and daughters of gods/goddesses have come down to Earth: to prove this fact.

Religion has always been a problem on the Earth. Religion will always evolve into a lie.

Religion is only a signpost of who is and what is, that's it!

Not anything else...

That is why you must know who you are!

Energy is all there is. Once this has become primary in the life, everything else will fall into place. Relationships, wealth, and success will come. I guarantee that.

If you want anything done, it will come from you. You're a god/goddess. I say this because we're energy and just by acknowledging that, you'll get to the place you need to get to. You will find your destiny, have a better relationship, get a new house, have children— whatever you desire. Acknowledge yourself as a god/goddess and see the miraculous results you get.

Everything you experience from this point onwards will be just that: experience.

Religion has always been a battleground, a struggle, for society, yet many people do not see the epidemic of violence it has caused – even today.

Many humans have killed other humans because of a difference in religion, different beliefs, different hair color, different skin color, different eye color, different nationalities, different clothes, different smells, ad infinitum. It's heartbreaking. It is an emotional ordeal because everyday someone dies because of the unconsciousness of another human being. But soon everything will be the way we seek the world to be and we will have peace on Earth...

From children to elders, many have been raped, slaughtered, hung, crucified, beaten, and even burned because of religion and being religious.

The same goes for animals. They're no different from anything else that breathes life such as us.

All these aspects of unconscious death leads to one thing only: loss of the mind, the control, and the power of others.

Let me talk a little about control and power:

Control and power are sort of intertwined with each other. They link together like a knot in a rope, and both are illusions.

How are both illusions?

The desire for power starts off in the mind and gradually begins seeking attention throughout the body. It gains attention from the ego.

For example, some people might begin their obsession with power by body building. People seek power of attraction and physical force by increasing the size of their muscles.

I know what you're thinking, "That's good. Wanting to get in shape is desirable." But the downfall occurs when you don't take control of your mind, which is telling you, "These muscles are awesome. Look how great I am." Then it can cause several misuses of the mind, such as starting to use steroids, self-infatuation, worship of others, or the sense of pride.

Those false images aren't the right tools for becoming prosperous or knowing who you are. Instead, it leads you to create a false idol of yourself.

You might even get attracted to others like wrestlers, boxers, and UFC fighters.

Others might become fond of you...

You might be thinking it's true love and that she or he is your real soul mate. The real reason is that the other person is attracted to your body, which has the power to get the attention of whoever is infatuated with fit bodies.

It is what you would call lust...

And then control comes with it.

If you ask me, it can be tantalizing. The control can turn you into a false idol for others.

A person might like a very massive and muscular person, but they're concerned only with the body, and that'll fail. It is a very conditional love. The object of this affection, in turn, is conditioned to love the control.

Control feeds the false sense of self, just as power does.

Without the power, control is nothing.

Have you ever tried to control your children?

Some might say, "No," or if you grew up like me, then you might say yes. If you have, then you'll know that if you tell them, "No. You can't have that," they might throw a tantrum.

Then you might say, "Go to your room" in a calming manner and the child might say, "No," again.

If you are unconscious (like I used to be), then raise your voice. As soon as the child hears the power in your voice (almost like thunder in a storm), he or she gets scared and runs swiftly across the room or cries. The unconscious you may feel pleased with the power.

The illusion of control needs power and vice-versa. They are both tied together.

That is why you have to know who you are before you can reach self-awareness and growth.

Once the illusion of power, control, and the false sense of establishing self in religion has been broken, then you can see a much better world. Imagine how much more beautiful this world would be without the egos and the different religions and the judgments and the killings. That's paradise waiting to happen. And believe me. We are on our way. The Earth will harbor peace.

When I used to attend church, I used to call myself as a Pentecostal. I got tired of that, and I switched churches. I became Baptist, then I switched churches again.

Every time I switched churches, I became the adherent of a different religion. They all teach the same lesson and study the same things—even praying to the same God. It didn't make a difference.

The only change was the way each pastor preached and the way each choir sang songs…

It was like joining a gang.

In some churches, many people worship the pastor. "Oh, the pastor said this and the pastor said that." People even feed off the way other people dress, pray, and shout. It seems like a circus, if you ask me.

Miracles happen when positive forces join; then healings happen. "You're healed." And that is all there is to it. This is the real understanding of who you are. Life is a piece of cake if you take nothing seriously, not even death. You live for death. Death is the evolution of consciousness. Without death, there'd be no life in the midst of death. An explosion happens, like a star that has reached its peak.

I watch so many documentaries on slavery and how hard slavery was. Do you know what the slaves did when they were on the plantations? They danced and prayed to God that one day they'd be free. I don't understand why, after they got free, they still danced and prayed to God about something. They prayed to see a long-lost family member, overcome a sickness, or whatever they wanted. Even to this day, they still do these acts as if it is really getting them somewhere. I do not want to pay too much attention to it because, if I pay attention to it, then it becomes my reality. Let just say that God does not grant wishes.

Now if God said to rest on the seventh day, then why would you attend a church just to hear what you already should know, then come home even crazier than you were?

Let your body rest—not just on what they call the Sabbath but—any day that you can.

Live your life healthy and stress free. Believe me. I know what it takes to work over forty hours a week, seven days a week, and sometimes two jobs, then have to get up for church on top of that. For what? To give money away that you worked so hard for? When your mortgage is due and you need help, will your church help you out then?

When you start to live your destiny, working will seem like drinking water. Time will pass quickly. You'll enjoy that feeling forever.

So when you work, it is really for eternity. Working is supposed to feel like bliss. When you are working through passion, you can do it all day and night. Not even sleep can stop you from working. Time ceases to exist.

Don't let religion get you caught up in believing in just one God. If God answered all your prayers for you, then what's the point of living? Suppose you pray to this being living in the clouds, jotting down your every move. To be honest, it is not really about that. God is not limited. We shouldn't put labels on God or on ourselves.

The more you rest, breathe, and be healthy, the quicker you can love yourself. Then you will attract others with the same ideals.

Become a servant to yourself and to others. By doing that, you create a god of yourself and more gods in others. This is what we are supposed to do. Nature isn't about work, work, and work until you're blue in the face.

It is about living and loving and spreading the unconditional love that we see in ourselves to others in whatever ways we can.

Do it with compassion and freedom; learn to understand the true nature of self; go to the inside of self and explore; and go on adventures to discover knowledge through meditation.

It is the only way to know that you're always a god/goddess and to know true wisdom born of ecstasy and true knowledge born of unmanifested thought.

Self-exploration will reveal any truth you seek. Try it and you too will be transformed and astonished at what the true self really is.

If you want wealth, go to the Supreme Self. If you want to be prosperous, go to the Supreme Self. If you want peace and to receive love from others, go to the Supreme Self. If you want to succeed in anything, just go to the Supreme Self. Explore and contemplate and soon you will see what you have in store for you and what is to soon become of you.

Your heart will guide you. It'll show you what you're to do: the correct steps you should take. You will also attract people to guide you to the next steps you need to take. Believe me. All this is true. Put it to the test. Follow your will.

You'll never let yourself down. You know exactly what you need to know to manifest your destiny. Do not let the ego empower you to a false destiny.

Sometimes, the reason we get ourselves in predicaments is simply because we let our minds take control of our lives. Individuals might believe they are talking and creating action on the next level of thought, but it's the mind doing what it's designed to do. The mind seeks reality, no matter what. So is this wrong? No. Of course not. But we must understand who is in charge.

Know who you are. Don't let religion get in the way of learning who is in control of you in this lifetime. And if you ask me, religion can also blind you if you don't know your true self. Religion can keep you from knowing yourself. Do not start believing in outside sources; instead, believe in the source within. You are a Consciousness.

The more you think about the negative past, the more you build up a negative person. Let go of whatever you need to let go of to move on to the next stage in life. Do not focus on the past or the future, since neither one can bring you to a place of stillness. Focus on the present moment—like, at this moment, you are reading this book.

Do not continue to focus on the past or present. Do not give the past power over your life. It should not become a big deal in your head. Do not let the past become your priority. Do not let the past become your reality. Prove that the idea that "history always repeats itself" is wrong.

That is why it seems like events that happen in this lifetime repeat themselves. People in this lifetime give life to the past by always focusing on the past—and that includes partaking in history lessons, studying the past, dwelling on the past, or even talking about old things that happened in the past with family members. It's all still recognizing and identifying with it. That leads the past to become your reality. It is all about attraction.

You're a magnet and you're constantly pulling events toward you. Whether you want to believe this or not, your actions will always determine your future.

The only reason you're pulling events toward you (positive or negative) is because you are made up of energy. This is the flow of life. That's why things come and then go. You have the day and then you have the night: today rain, tomorrow snow. But who knows? Life is not meant for us to know. Life was created out of the unknown. The only reason we're here is to create a world we can enjoy. Everybody is responsible for creating their own Heaven.

Deep down inside, I know that you can sense this. Truth always emerges from love. The words you are reading on this page—and on every other page in this book—are words of love, compassion, bliss, ecstasy, and oneness.

The more attention you give the past, the less focus you give to right now.

Always remember this: "There can be too many problems and chaos. You try too often to create a future out of past problems. Too often, you link to the false sense of self."

4

Relationships and Understanding Self...

I laugh at opposition to same sex marriage. I mean how can you not accept same sex marriage? Relationships are not meant to be for just men and women, but for all spirits that feel affection for each other. Love is our natural state of being.

Whether it is men and men, women and women, or women and men, there's no difference. That is the way the god/goddess works. Believe it or not. We all put limitations on God and say this or that is wrong. But who really knows what gods/goddesses like? Just ask around. We are gods and goddesses.

God is everyone and everybody. God is the epitome of our existence. God is the voice that travels through person to person, waiting for someone to listen. God doesn't judge, condemn, or discriminate. God doesn't rule anyone. If your "God" is not like this, then change your God—or, more accurately, change yourself.

God does not have a label. God is all, so why put a label on it? That is something to think about. Look all around you. You will see nothing but chaos if you label everything. Now see everything as yourself.

Instantly, the beauty comes out. You'll no longer judge, harm, or torment another creature.

God is feeling, if you ask me: feeling from the inside of self.

God is the embodiment of this world and universe. That's the way God works. That's why we've mystics and prophets who tell us the many revelations of what and who's to come. They're so immersed with spirit and the universe that they become unified to the is-ness of life. They understand the totality of which they are...

God is every being that moves and breathes. From the clouds in the air, to the twinkle in the sky, God is every mold and molecule and disease we find hazardous to this society...

God is all!

We slaughter animals and wonder why the flu goes around. We cut down and kill rainforests and wonder why wild fires are destroying houses. Our cars constantly burn to move, and we wonder why we've more cold days than hot days—wonder why the icecaps in the artic areas are melting.

It's all because we're taking advantage of the Earth. Earth doesn't belong to us; it belongs to itself...

You've trained your mind to think mine, mine, mine, instead of accepting it as is, is, is...

The human mind can take you to a place where you can lose your sense of who you are if you do not know your true way of being. Realize you are here to recreate.

People commit suicide because everything can be overwhelming and hectic at times...

Soon, we will all see the Earth take back what belongs to it. Paradise will be reconstructed.

Maybe it'll take thousands or millions of years, but we don't really know how long it'll take...

That is the reason for tsunamis happening in certain areas of the world. That is why the icecaps are melting in the arctic. That's why volcanic eruptions are happening around the world. That is why earthquakes are occurring in new areas. Earth is reconstructing herself, and we're here to experience it as it happens.

Please do not put any limitations on god. We do not know all the angles of God. We think we do, but we really don't. That is why, to this day, we still can't explain the nature of space.

Space is undefined and leads to so many un-manifested beliefs about God. We, as humans, are the same way. He or she is undefined. You can't fit an analogy to anything, not even same sex marriage. It is not all about creation; it's about love too. That is the secret key to the life we are.

Love all, no matter who they are—or what they are—because the veil masking other sentient beings in the universe, aliens, will be lifted soon.

Right now, we're not ready for that. We think we're the only creatures who can think, and we're not so sure about others. If we can't accept ourselves, what makes you think we're going to accept other beings?

Relationships can be difficult to handle, especially if you still associate yourself with a negative past.

What I mean is, say, for instance, you were raped and physically abused as a child. Those emotions and scars live on until you break free of them. If you refuse to allow your past to drop away, you're going to attract unhealthy men and women who'll treat you as a victim. If that is what you see in yourself, you will make that reality happen.

Know that events are learning opportunities. To have a life, you must live a life. In order to teach, you must have something to teach.

We are like magnets. We send out magnetic signals, negative or positive. We're vibrating every Nano-second with high and low frequencies. Some vibrate at higher frequencies than others. Reality will reflect the frequencies at which we vibrate. Whatever you put out, that shall be your world. This is the law of the universe.

We need to break out of the habit of letting our minds get the best of us, or even get ahead of us. We must start thinking positively, no matter what situation we are in. That is also the key to living a successful life:

Having a positive mind gets you positive results.

We must change our thinking patterns. As I said earlier, we're attracting every situation to our lives.

The key to changing the world is to change your thinking, and the key to beginning that process is stillness...

What you send out is what you get back. Whatever mood you're in is whatever reality you'll be in. If you're joyful all the time, no matter what, then your reality will produce happy moments all the time. If you're depressed or angry all the time, then your reality will reflect that. That will be your natural state of being until you decide that you've had enough suffering.

Every day, hour, minute, and second, we're creating who we are and also creating our world. If we continue to stay unconscious of ourselves, then we'll never see a change in relationships, society, or even this Earth.

Some people look for love, instead of loving themselves first.

If you do not love yourself, then why would you try to seek a relationship? You will inflict emotional problems on the one you love.

In other words, what you feel on the inside of yourself, you'll produce externally. The effects of what you feel—no matter who appears in your reality—will influence others.

That's why the world is in the predicament that it's in now. Negativity spreads, like a disease. The cycle continues and continues and continues until somebody steps out of the pattern and breaks it. But it all starts with you.

Life should be lived for fun and self-exploration. We're supposed to rejoice in our existence. After all, we can do so much, be whoever we want to be, go wherever we want to go—in short, we've free will!

Marriage is intended for two people to be joined as one. But we need to love ourselves first, and then spread the joys ourselves with others. There's nothing wrong with spending the rest of your life with the person you care for. However, you should value yourself. If, at any moment, you decide to change who you are, then your spouse should not harm you. He or she ought to respect your inner evolution.

Everyone must reach—or should be reaching for—this level of consciousness. Everyone must understand the evolution of the mind. Things don't stay the same, including your thinking. Everything evolves—and I mean everything. So, with that said, you should attract people who are like you (on a conscious level), then you won't have any problems or confusions in your home or world.

If you are in an unconscious relationship and suddenly you try to change your way of thinking to better yourself, then believe me: If your spouse doesn't agree—or isn't on the same level of consciousness—there will be problems!

An unconscious person cannot withstand a conscious-minded person. There's no attraction: like attracts like, positive attracts positive, and negative attracts negative...

On a deeper level, the other person can't complete you. You complete you. The other person can't decide the evolution of your mind.

You were born in this world as one person, and you'll leave this world alone. So why would you get married for the long term without doing anything with your life first? You're going to cause harm to the other person, simply because of the you are incomplete.

There're so many worldly marriages that're so funny and crazy. It is hilarious.

People get too bound up in their relationships to make the other person happy. If you're not happy, then you'll never be able to spread happiness to another person. It all begins with you.

For instance, there're people who have been abused mentally and physically; there're people who are too submissive; and there're people who get in a relationship just to cover up their feelings for the opposite sex. They're ashamed and/or afraid of who they are. You shouldn't ever feel that way. We're God recreating who we are every second, minute, and hour...

Worldly marriages can be a blessing, a burden, a joyous experience to some, a curse to many, but, for whatever reason, marriage is not intended for this life unless you're doing a deal of some sort etc.....

Just follow your feelings, and you will know what your next move is.

Some marriages and relationships will force you to lose the truest understanding of who you are, which is God. And nobody should tolerate losing their godliness.

I'm not saying that you shouldn't be looking for a companion in life. If that is what you want to do, then do it. Just be aware of the other person's thinking pattern. See if it compares to your thinking. Remember to be in the present moment.

Do whatever makes you happy. If you're in a relationship or married, however, and that person wants you to put on a mask—to change who you are—to put you in a predicament where you have to change certain things about yourself, then I believe you should first talk about it. Then, if there is no improvement, that's when it's time to call it quits.

Well, how do I know if what I am doing is correct?

Go by your feelings. That's what you have to do—in order to know what's the right choice in everything you do. Feel it and a lot of times, the first choice is the best choice. Understand the second and the third choices, but once you hear the first choice, go with it and don't second guess.

We must know that everybody on the face of this Earth is trying to find themselves in many ways. True gods/goddesses know this, whether it is being with the opposite sex, same sex, or with yourself.

Do not lose yourself trying to make other people happy. Happiness must emerge from within...

If they are not happy with themselves and you thought that you could help that person, then it is time to move on. Don't waste time. Spend your time wisely...

Remember that unconditional love is the key to every relationship and marriage.

If marriage is what you want to do, then do not judge. Even though you're in a relationship or married, you're still trying to find out who you are. There's something that needs to be learned. It's up to you to figure out what that is. You create your reality always. Nobody can ever create your reality but you.

If marriage—or being in a relationship—is what is required of you at this time in your life, then do not reject it. Follow the path of least resistance. You will know what to do and the next step to take. Feel it.

When it comes down to relationships or marriages, if neither party trusts the other: not communicating, being selfish, keeping themselves apart, then it simply won't work.

Being in any relationship is an act of communion with the other person. Understand the other. Both parties should be on the same level of growth and respect. The minute one falls out of oneness with self, change will begin. Whether it is a good or bad change, it'll start. Know yourself. Once you know who you truly are, then you can make the choice of being in a relationship or not...

5

Control of the Mind

Control of the mind, or being still with one's self, is something that I've been waiting to discuss. This is what caused me to "tell the world."

I believe that we, human beings, really need to stop and meditate about what we're focusing on in this reality.

Is the mental noise in our heads mistaken for our identity?

Who is that person?

Is it the ego or the true self?

We need to escape the mental noise. We may think that it's normal for us to have this mental noise in our heads, but I'm telling you it isn't.

We've lost control of our thinking. We're now trying to get it back. There's been too much chaos spread amongst people that did not even deserve it. Unconsciousness is a disease.

The noise in our head that we see as normal in this reality is only the perception of our minds. The mind tries to deal with this reality—or should I say this Earth?—and as each day goes by, the mind takes the place of you. The mind takes over your body and you see yourself as what your mind sees you as. The mind will convince you that you are a person, an animal, the opposite sex, teacher, minister, mom, or dad. Your mind will paint you based on your desires to get married, become president, explore opposites sexes, or even take over the world.

What I'm trying to say here is that this noise that we mistake for our true selves is only the subconscious mind going too far with unconscious thinking. The mind is always at work, trying to discover whatever it can pick up and attach itself to. It has to keep moving and keep looking for a reason to judge. It does not do this because it wants to, but because it needs to. The mind is designed to survive. It creates problems, so it can solve them.

How can we stop this from happening?

How can we escape this organ that's encapsulating this world and perpetuating the destruction of humanity?

There is nothing we can do, but deal with it in a conscious way. There are numerous ways to do this. One method is meditation. And if you ask me, this is probably the only step to consciousness. But, I admit, it varies for many people. Meditation betters the human race. It helps the mind evolve the way it is supposed to evolve: by self-reflection.

Like I mentioned earlier, this world is going in a very peculiar way. I believe that it won't get any better, because anyone who constantly judges (which is to say, tries to survive) can become conscious. But there's too much suffering for everyone to awaken.

This is the nature of the mind. Becoming aware of this positive nature of humanity is empowering on its own. You can break away from the false sense of the person you were. 99% of the time, when you do become aware of this, you were probably in the worst predicament of your life, in a near death experience, or just going through some hard times.

We all have a desire to be who we are—and not who we think we are or have been forced to become.

We've that itch for freedom that comes with just the thought or smell of peace. We've this deep knowing that we're God. That's the truth for you, and the deeper person within knows this. You can't run from it, nor can you hide from it, and if you don't get it in this lifetime, then, in some lifetime or another, you'll realize this truth. We all will realize this truth eventually.

Everywhere you look, there's hate, killing, politics, poverty, people starving—plenty of events are taking place that cause human misery. And it's only because we don't have control over our minds, because we don't know that we're God. Because, if we did, then none of the turmoil that we cause would exist.

Everything that we see on TV and around us is designed to keep us lost in unconsciousness. That's why we, as pure light beings, should pay attention to what's around us.

We need to pay attention to what we watch on the TV and how we treat others. We don't see or even put ourselves in anybody else's shoes but our own. We have lost touch with empathy. Being that way is selfish. It is evil. It leads you to the destruction of love.

Earth was made from God's love. After all we've been through on Earth, we still have forgotten that. We have forgotten that love for all—including the ones that we once hated—is one of the most important lessons to learn in this lifetime. Most importantly, we've forgotten who we are, where we came from, and even our divine name.

Unconscious thinking leads you to the loss of love and peace for yourself. And as you continue to go deeper into unconsciousness, you lose touch with true nature, which is one with self. That's also why we're trapped in fear, anxiety, greed, selfishness, hate, etc. because there is no stillness in the body. Stillness is the voice of God.

When there is no stillness in the body, everything else becomes a poison....

We need to practice controlling our minds and staying conscious of our surroundings, as the animals, insects, trees, and plants do. We need to practice being present here on Earth. We are a gift to the Earth. We are precious to this planet, whether we know it or not.

"We are the world." (Michael Jackson).

Meditation is a great way of controlling the mind and breaking away from the negative veil of life and false sense of self. I believe mediation will end a lot of the turmoil caused by human behavior.

It will also end the hate, fear, greed, and selfishness that embrace the Earth.

Without stillness in the body, chaos takes control.

When chaos takes form, it may already be too late. You have to cut it off at the root, which is hate of one's self. We must prevent the spread of this virus, this anger that we've built up from the past and sometimes from the present as well. Stop resisting the present moment. Allow it to be.

A state of awareness of this kind sounds impossible, but only if you're outside looking in. And then only because the mind can't picture a reality that's devoid of chaos… The mind is programmed to survive chaos, so it rejects its dismissal.

This is the true awareness in store for humanity: not letting the mind take you over.

What you've done is you've built yourself up to be this person who, according to you, is real. You might think the person you were was real, but, in fact, it wasn't. You have to live with the mind that you've identified as yourself since the day you were born.

You were taught to believe in a God or many gods and goddesses. You were taught to act according to society for the validation of self. You were taught to attend institutions of holiness for self-approval. With all the indoctrination you've absorbed over the years, I've a piercing question for you: Is that the real you?

What do I know about me?

How much of me do I know on my own?

Everything you've done before you started reading this book, you've done it with complete noise. That is why things never work out, because when you complete a level of life with noise, you must do it all over again. You have not learned what it means to complete reality, with absolute stillness. It is like you must re-read a paragraph of a book because you did not interpret it carefully enough. The mind and body were in control of you, so chaos will keep happening and will keep on repeating itself. End the cycle.

Some people wait until death to understand that they're the Universal Self, but by then it's too late. You'll have to do it all over again. That's the reality of your situation. You must keep riding this train until you see the is-ness of life, as some may call it.

Life is sort of like a video game. You do not move on to the next level until you get it. Most people must go through many, many lifetimes before they can let go of whatever is needed. Past lifetimes are learning experiences, but the key is to not give up. Keep living until it finally clicks.

"When the understanding of your will becomes the will of all"

This is one unified process. Being unconscious prevents the process. Instead of everybody working as one unit, we're all divided and not spreading the unconditional love of our universal true selves to anyone.

Hate should hurt you to the point of wanting to regurgitate. Anger should get you to the point of needing meditation because your head should hurt so bad from the negative energy that you feel. Unconsciousness numbs you to everything. That is a dangerous situation. Unconsciousness should sicken us. And maybe it does.

Everywhere you look, there's danger. Nobody cares about anybody. When you walk down the street and see the exact same being or, as I call it, yourself in the mirror, there's silence and no communication—not even a simple, "Hello," nod, or gesture.

It might be because they are in a different clique. It might even be because of their race. Maybe they are taller or shorter than you. But whatever the circumstance, that is not the real humanity. Let us all wake up from this dream of unconsciousness. It is destroying the world. It is a serial killer. That is why you and I are here to "tell the world."

We all have to tell the world about this new way of living, this new way of life—a life without pain, suffering, sickness, egotistic behavior, money, conflicting government parties, taxes, institutions of any kind, hunger, worries, jealousies, whippings, or abuse of any form or type. There will be no room for any type of negativity. Can you imagine a life like that? If so, then let's all make it happen. We come together to create this narrative.

We all may or may not see this, but consciousness starts with me and you. It begins with your neighbor, your enemy, even the "strangers" you walk past in supermarkets.

The unconditional love that is inside each last one of us is there to show you who you truly are.

You do not receive this truth from your spouse, kids, family members, or institutions of any kind. You are everything. Why wouldn't you use a resource so immense and immediate?

You're the person who has come from that broken home; you're the person who has been homeless; you're the person who is getting married; you're the person who is getting a divorce; you're the person who's been through hurricane Rita and Katrina too; you're the person who's been through the tsunami disaster; you're the person who's rescued people in absolute disarray; you're the person who doesn't care about anybody or anyone; you're the person who said "No" to a another person who's less fortunate than you; you're the person who's lost your job or been jobless for years due to economic struggles; you're the person who has to be a stripper just to make ends meet; you're the person who's living next door; you're the person who caused that terrible accident; you're the person who killed an infant or child; you're the person who lost their legacy; you're the person who's doing the killings around the nation; you're the person who's gossiping to others; you're the person who's raping another person; you're the person who's been raped; you're the person who's the counselor for rape victims; you're the person who has broken away from everything you were taught by past generations; you're the person who's been enlightened by another person; you're the person who's teaching enlightenment; you're the person who has become conscious of self; you're the person who's realized that true being is sparkling throughout truth and wisdom; and you're that person who's realized that you're God.

Know that you're God. Don't be afraid of what anybody may say to you; just know that, and let your heart guide your decision. Then, your destiny will be born...

Know yourself...

Who are you?

Who's the person that's doing the thinking? Who is asking these questions?

Are you the question from which questions emerge?

There's mysticism about this and when you meditate on this question, you're empowered to the degree of nothingness...

This degree of nothingness to the average thinking mind of today will not be able to meditate on this level. There's nothing to talk about. Only love in the heart of self can comprehend at this level of stillness.

The key is to know who you are. Go to that place of stillness within the mind, that place you thought never existed. Through your eyes, you perceive your world through your thoughts.

So, what am I saying?

You must still the mind immediately. The quicker you do this, the better. The universe will wait until you make up your mind as to which direction you want to go. The second you decide, then the universe begins to open up all the doors. All obstacles are instantly pushed out of the way. You can enjoy who you are, stress free. And all of this is done through the stillness and meditation.

That is why it is important to still the mind as often as possible. You want your thoughts to be pure and not be of the flesh. You want what you perceive through your eyes to match what you perceive through meditation.

Who are you?

Again, I ask who you are. Nobody knows who they really are. Many people believe that they're their bodies—living, breathing, moving, thinking, doing things that seem to make them feel better—but is this who you really are? Is this the entity that you feel you should be?

If there're doubts within the heart when meditating on this question through stillness within the mind and body, there should be changes without you saying or thinking anything.

The mind begins to shift and, suddenly, thoughts begin to be clearer. But, like I said, change must come from within. To start that process, you have to still the mind and body. You will not know who you really are until you begin to practice stillness.

Practicing stillness will elevate the mind beyond the body. Soon, the true essence of you will begin to express itself without you even knowing the process. It just happens. That is the beauty of living: allowing the essence of your being to evolve each and every day. And it just takes one breathe at a time.

We are all in such a hurry. It seems like nobody wants to "stop and think." They teach you this in preschool, yet most people still operate in the mind-made self. Most people still operate in selfishness instead of selflessness. Most people view themselves as this living species which wants to dominate everything. We forget how small we really are compared to our solar system and to the universe.

We, as beings of light, should've already been ready. Pure consciousness is bound to be forever acknowledged. There's no excuse not to act. For the gods and goddesses have been getting the attention of everyone. We will have peace on Earth. This is the destiny of humanity. We, as beings of eternal light, need to get a grasp of this concept. We need to stop living the delusion that we are our bodies. That's the wrong answer. That is not the correct way of living. That's a strike against ourselves.

Stillness, slow to speak, and "love for all" is the truth in man. This evolution of consciousness dwells in every heart. Why anybody would choose not to listen to this inner God voice, I do not know. Maybe people are addicted to themselves. We're all light in the form of matter. We won't ever be disconnected from the source. It's impossible to be disconnected; we're forever eternal light.

We must sharpen our DNA through meditation so our children can be born of universal intelligence. We must ensure the evolution of our species and bring about our angelic form of this great Heaven. Now is the time to break away from every false habit that we thought was the norm. Be focused on your inner light. This may sound crazy, but the insanity of killing ourselves ought to be more alarming.

How dare we say that this type of consciousness doesn't exists? If this consciousness didn't exists, we wouldn't exists. The words in this book wouldn't exist. The Earth would not exist.

The blueprint of our existence resides in each and every last one of us. It's up to us to bring forth a new species of human being—species that can fly and soar to experience every angle and viewpoint of existence. Our new human race will experience grander ways of intelligence in coming lifetimes.

It must start now. If we beings of light continue to wait, we will forfeit our true evolution to the highest levels of creation. There's Heaven on Earth, and we keep rejecting it. But as the planets begin to align, as our universe continues to expand, deep consciousness will require no breathing at all. The Earth will begin to lose oxygen in the generations to come. The only beings to tolerate this experience will be light-beings.

We're to express our true nature at all times, while enjoying this dissolving of the third dimensional reality. It's a pleasure to experience this transition from Earth to Heaven. "This is it." We are experiencing a cosmic change in our reality. We need to take every advantage of this change.

Everything that we see, touch, taste, and smell is becoming a harder vibration as the years go by, and these harder vibrations are being intensified due to the expansion of our universe. Intellect is being born at a rapid pace that can be only understood while being still. Our bodies are transforming into light entities to expel more light to the Earth as she begins to lose all love for us. Therefore, some of us may experience more joy and love than others. Any individual who acknowledges this truth in themselves will activate wisdom, love, and prosperity. The environment will "mirror their reality."

Can't you sense the aliveness in what you're reading? That feeling of aliveness comes from the cosmic rays that hit you day in and day out. That aliveness is the activation of the soul. Whatever you say or do at the point of aliveness, that's when reality is born.

There's a reshaping of our DNA structure. The reshaping begins in our consciousness. This can't be ignored any longer. We, as "beings of light," say that we want Heaven on Earth, but we don't expect this in our reality. Why is this so? Focusing on the problem will never get us anywhere near to the solution. The question is within each last one of us.

This reshaping will happen, no matter what. This is the beginning of our eternal way of living. There's no turning back. Everything, including our evolution, moves forward. It is impossible to go back. Possibilities only seem backwards when one experiences death. Our way of life is life. Our knowing of the knowing is eternal. We're experiencing the changing of the guards. This is a miraculous change in our human species. What a ride we're in for! Everything is okay. Nothing can ever diminish our eternal fate of the here and now. Every moment is the present moment always. That statement alone should be a wakeup call. This lack of knowledge is unacceptable. We, as humankind, can't allow to slip up again. We must stop creating misery and insanity for one another all over again.

"For the lack of one's self is the root of all unconsciousness/evil..."

Are we intelligence birthed to unintelligence?

We suffer this lack of knowledge until we are light essence, which is the most powerful essence. It is forever a part of you. It bursts out of you, through the union of mind, body, and soul.

The fact that we're born here and forget the true essence of who we are is the result of mistaken identity. Without that, what happens to us wouldn't happen. If we already knew who we were, then there wouldn't be any point to our lives. There would be no need to experience anything, since everything would be known.

Everything about the human species keeps on changing and reshaping and changing and reshaping. We keep on evolving. Through this, we decide what we feel about ourselves. We ought to judge this based on our actions.

"Our actions are our impressions of what we feel."

We decide—through every event that's born through our thinking—how we feel about ourselves. So we may express anger; we may express confusion; we may express happiness, and so on…

You see, we can't appreciate evolution because we aren't patient enough. We can't see in 360°. We may depend on the outside sources of today's world such as television or attaching ourselves to people, instead of going with the feelings on the inside of self that enable us to know and understand the ultimate light source that we are.

The fact that we cannot see ourselves is a great mystery. It teaches us to always love from the inside out, because outside appearance is always subject to change. Love is unchangeable. It teaches us to respect and love others.

You are reading this book. Something brought you to this place right here and right now. What's that something that brought you here and now? I think it is your true vibration, which vibrates constantly to get your attention of who you really are. Know that you're not your body, nor are you the perception of thoughts that constantly run through the mind. You're the complete knower. You are aware of the awareness of you knowing who you are.

This knowledge is real and blissful, but you have to stop resisting life. Once you do, everything will begin to become clearer. You'll begin to look around and feel the energy and vibration that's in control of the complete knowing. The ecstasy of that, you cannot ever run away from.

The controller is you. You control life. And you control death. But without the knowledge of being the controller, you give power to outside sources that (you feel) are not connected with you. Do not go on living without knowing your true intelligence. You can stop, listen, and figure it all out, just by not judging anything, just by not giving anything a name. Everything you see is the total perception of your thoughts. Your thoughts are the power of your reality. So again: Know yourself. Still yourself. Realize that you're the creator of life and death, good and evil, poverty and success. Control your mind.

I want to end this book by saying that I did not know that this book was going in the direction that it went. I'm now Thirty-Three Years of age. I started writing this at twenty-four, so this was a short process. Some might think that is a long time, but I believe that it all happened as it should. I'm so grateful for my growth through writing this book. I know, with my feelings, that many will read this book and judge me, but many will also read this book and say, "It's about time." Now is the time for everyone to start to realize who they truly are and learn to express their true divinity within themselves. We are all one, and this oneness is an ongoing process of our evolution.

If we do not demolish the continuous process of unhealthy thinking—and use thought the way that thought should be used—then egos are created, and we all begin to die. We're not the body. We aren't the mind. We're the true energy that controls this reality. We're here as beings of eternal light to have fun and enjoy this ongoing process of what we call life.

6

Who are you?

I'm not saying that I'm perfect. I'm saying that we're all perfect. To understand this, you must experience not being perfect. How would we have the word, "perfect," without its antithesis? The ignorance of what's going on is an epidemic of eternal confusion within our untamed minds. Divide the lie from the truth. Truth is born from the un-manifested Supreme Self.

Who are you?

Are you a victim of cancer? Are you a victim of AIDs? Are you a pimp? Are you a pastor of a church? Are you a mother or father? Are you a sister or a brother? Are you the name you are born with? Are you the seeker or the knower? Are you all or the Supreme Self?

I say (vibration, energy, light), as a matter of fact, that all of these could be correct. They also could be wrong. It depends on how you feel. Feeling is the first indication of who you are, which is more than likely a vibration. The higher your vibration, the higher your consciousness. You can describe yourself as anything for the good or for the bad, but just follow how you feel in choosing so. Most beings will not even do that because of the repercussions in the Supreme Self's existence.

Many are called, but few are chosen. Why are they chosen? They follow their hearts and the feelings that is inside of them. Again, always live for that feeling. It is the Supreme Self getting your attention. Allow your true nature to be bestowed upon Gaia, for the reclamation of all. Ask yourself, "Do I really follow my heart in every choice I make and every action I commit?" If "No" comes to mind, then it is time to make a change. That change starts with you monitoring your every thought, good or bad.

You must be very careful because thoughts are vibrations. Each thought can contribute to your life. Acknowledge that thought. Then, look for how you feel. Search for the feeling behind it. Know that negative vibrations caused by thought can be very dangerous, so be cautious. That's why certain people can be at the wrong place, at the wrong time. As you do this more and more, it becomes second nature. Now you have the upper hand on every outcome or event that enters your presence.

This way of being is perfectly normal. People just do not practice it, so it sounds immoral, crazy, or even impossible to do. Knowing our true nature and acting it out is the way to live. What the human species acts out nowadays is very hazardous to the health of ourselves and the planet. Think about it: The average being is actively thinking minute after minute, hour after hour, day after day, and the only time in which you're not actively thinking is when you're sleeping. But then, when you awake (and I am talking physically waking up), the same constant thinking continues.

What you may not know is that your breathing is constantly and rapidly increasing or decreasing, depending on the conversation you may be having. If you are experiencing danger of some sort, fear anger is roused. Anger can be a very dangerous state of mind, because not only do you strike the opposing person with hurtful words, but you also put yourself at risk of heart disease, heart attack, and even stroke. The average person may believe that these emotions are normal, a natural way of life, but they aren't. Emotions like that produce misfortune in our lives. Negative actions create negative vibrations, and produce more negative events. Anger is something the individual picks up through certain events in life and so may believe that anger is normal. Let me put it this way: anger can be seen as an overload of the mind. It leads to a quick death and an unhealthy life. When you eliminate anger, you are one step closer to knowing who you are.

What we, as beings of this world, need to realize is that our thoughts are the way to this world and universe. Whatever we think about, we bring about. That's the key: Thought is energy. We give out energy and perceive energy, and this is constant day in and day out. It does not stop. A tree loses its leaves in the fall, but then grows new ones in the spring. We are born with power. Power is how we manifest our destiny. Without power, we wouldn't have a destiny. We would not exist in this moment without it. We are all supposed to use power for the greater good of all of humanity, but many people have different agendas. Greed has taken control of some, but not all. But it is all okay. We still have time. Yet time is running out. Our whole existence is power, and this power is energy. We breathe in energy and we breathe out energy. Our brains transmute energy to our whole body—and the body, itself, is energy. This is the power. We're born with energy. This entire universe operates on energy. Once this knowledge becomes second nature, life as we know it expands. We begin to operate on the same level and vibration as the universe. This is who we are (energy in manifested form).

We're walking, breathing, living stars, experiencing this lifetime with as much freedom and love as possible. We await our supernova, because this is who we are.

We're this continuous process that'll never end. It may end on this plane, but life will be experienced in many, many forms, on many,

many worlds, and in many, many universes. We're still at the beginning process of our evolution, and that won't end either. But what will end is the process of ignorance, of not propelling ourselves into the intellectual era of the Supreme Self.

For good or bad, for better or worse, this process of unconditional love will not ever end.

For we're what we are, experiencing this moment: the "present moment."

This moment is eternal thought at a standstill, erupting into events through our will. Again, this is still the beginning; everything must "evolve" to become love. "For he who holds the formula of love holds the entire universe." He or she who holds that knowledge close to his or her heart will start to understand the complete knowledge of the Universal Self—not controlling others with this power, but spreading the power like a virus, traveling through sources of compelled thinking.

This is the knowledge that resides in all of us and our true way of being. We'll conquer. We're the Supreme Self, fulfilling this prophecy with gratitude, unconditional love, power, eternal health, and finally wisdom.

We will impart this gift to Earth as she continues to pulse vibrant melodies into our hearts. She will survive humanity's greed, hate, jealously, division, lying, and dysfunction in this present reality. Now is the time to take back our lives and express our eternal love. We are gods with different languages and personalities, skin-color and living in different parts of the world.

We're eternal light that's aware of thought, body, and action. We produce the right decisions with words unveiled through wisdom, spreading through this reality, creating beauty and peace.

True self-awareness emerges when all of us reflect inward to find that the outside world is a product of our collective minds. So, yes, this is who we are. We're the Supreme Self, contained in human bodies. We share this reality together. We write this story together. So let us all tell the world together.

CPSIA information can be obtained
at www.ICGtesting.com
Printed in the USA
FFOW02n1601160718
47409897-50617FF